The Disappearing Trick

The Disappearing Trick

Poems by

Len Roberts

University of Illinois Press

Urbana and Chicago

Library of Congress Cataloging-in-Publication Data
Roberts, Len, 1947–
The disappearing trick : poems / by Len Roberts.
p.   cm.
ISBN-13: 978-0-252-03128-1 (cloth : acid-free paper)
ISBN-10: 0-252-03128-8 (cloth : acid-free paper)
ISBN-13: 978-0-252-07374-8 (pbk. : acid-free paper)
ISBN-10: 0-252-07374-6 (pbk. : acid-free paper)
I. Title.
PS3568.O2389D57   2007
811'.54—dc22   2006029373

Acknowledgments

My thanks to the editors of the following journals in which some of these poems, in various versions, first appeared:

The American Poetry Review: "I blame it on him," "Letter to HC in the Hospital," "My Old Friend, My Daughter, October, Wassergass," "Window Candle," "Letter #3 to Carruth about the Heron," "Monitoring Impulses," "The saints always"

Atlanta Review: "Washing the Steps"

Barrow Street: "Cover Girl Sparkle"

Boulevard: "The Eternal Present of the Ancient Chinese Poems," "The Chasm," "Four-Way Switch," "Limbo, Wassergass"

College English: "Card Game"

Five Points: "Right after Mass"

The Gettysburg Review: "Bullfrog, Wassergass"

The Georgia Review: "Pear Tart"

Gulf Coast: "My Father, Setting the Line, Sunny October," "Considering Aunt Bea's white Toyota Celica"

The Hudson Review: "Window of Our Soul"

The Kenyon Review: "Flicking" (Published as "Flicking the Switch")

Mad Poets Review: "Receiving at the Kneeling Rail," "Peaches in Pennsylvania Late August"

Margie: an American Journal of Poetry: "Inside the dim kitchen the rosary," "What does a man who's 55 say"

Meridian: "Car on the Road, Late July, Wassergass"

Mid-American Review: "Lucky"

Ohio Review: "The Silent Archangels," "The Right Dress"

One-Trick Pony: "The Disappearing Trick"

The Paterson Literary Review: "Dinner with My Son, Casey Lynn's Diner, Hellertown"

Poetry: "Our Son Leaves His Miniature Japanese Sand Garden Behind Because There Will Be No Room in the Dorm," "I CAN'T FORGET YOU."
Poetry International: "Sequence," "In the Expert Valet Clothing Shop"
Poetry Northwest: "Hanging Tinsel"
Prairie Schooner: "MISSING"
River Styx: "Indulgences for the Dead," "Fireflies at the Cohoes Drive-In," "Poison Sumac"
The Southern Review: "A Room for Jesus," "Pitching in the Aggie," "Snowflakes in Hell"
Virginia Quarterly Review of Literature: "Sleep-Eaze," "Heaven's Gate"

My thanks also to the editors of the following anthologies or textbooks where some of these poems, in various versions, appeared:

Atlanta Review, International Publication Prize Winner in Poetry 2004 International Poetry Competition: "Washing the Steps"
A Man's World: an International Anthology of Male Poetry, University of Georgia Press, 2005: "I blame it on him"
Lasting: Poems on Aging, Pima Press, 2005: "Monitoring Impulses"
Naming the World, Heinemann, 2005: "I CAN'T FORGET YOU."
Never Before: Poems about First Experiences, Milkweed Editions, 2005: "Window of Our Soul"
River Styx 2006 International Poetry Contest: "Poison Sumac"

My special thanks goes to Ken Fifer and Larry Lieberman for their tremendously helpful comments about many of these poems.

For Joshua

Contents

V

I

Washing the Steps

I was washing the hallway steps
with a sopped blue sponge and a bucket
   of clouded water
   and she was coming after,
rubbing her thumb hard from side
   to side,
holding the dirt-smudged whirls up
with last night's lipstick-stained smile
   that said *Begin again at the top*
and this time work your way down right—

so as I sit on the padded chair,
waxy faces floating by, nodding,
whispering words I can't quite hear,
a woman placing a hankie in my hand
   almost makes me rise
   to dust my mother's casket off,
   where the others left their smudged
fingerprints without a second thought,

me half-expecting her to open those eyes
   that saw every grit and mote,
for her to lift that thumb again to rub
   the coffin's solid walnut grain,
tell me to go fill the bucket with some
   warm suds
and the thick, heavy-duty sponge,
to put some heart into it this time,
   to *bear down, bear down,*
   till the shine comes up.

My Old Friend, My Daughter, October, Wassergass

Quadruple bypass, rows of pills that would have killed a horse,
    daughter dead of cancer,
son living alone behind his house in a cold trailer, my old friend
is still eating store-bought apple pie and cursing the crust,
he's still doing some writing and maybe even some fucking,
    living right in his Syracusean nights,
what with his new Xerox machine, Oxy-Pac and satellite dish
I'd been telling him for years to get so he could finally bring in
    a decent picture of the basketball games,
renovated, he might call himself, *new-fangled, all get-up,*
just a few of those catchy Vermont phrases he'd stored up in a madness

    I don't even want to think about,
not with a father and brother gone like that,
not with a daughter on Paxil and Prozac
and God knows what else the shrink might send home in one of those
    white packages all marked
with blue letters and numbers that tell her mother and me
    two now, three later,
my friend's story of cowering in an attic when his high school band
    played down the street
not so far from our daughter banging away at her guitar for hours,
refusing to go to school, refusing to answer the phone,
the one lawn chair set out in the barn by the hay door where she
    sits at night to watch the field,
the occasional car passing a few hundred feet down on Wassergass Road,
    all that blackness in her mind

making me nod my head the way my old friend nodded his once
    in Maine when I visited him,
Proust on the table, the loon moaning with a crescent moon,

my friend moving like a shadow in the kitchen to boil us some water
    for tea,
the bottle of Bushmills slammed on the table to remind him
of what he could not do, until he did, and then could not stop,
the way my daughter cannot stop, the doctor said, shaking
until whatever seizes her has passed, anxiety, dread,
    an aloneness almost impossible to comprehend,
sixteen and already frozen when she looks up at the stars
so clear now in autumn where the air has turned cold
    and the big, green walnut pods
keep thud, thud, thudding to the hardening ground.

I blame it on him

when I'm a quarter-inch off
    and the molding won't fit
no matter how hard I hammer it,
and when the outlet goes dead,
    it's his fumbling hands
trying to sort green from white
    from black
while I shout at my wife
    to call an electrician
even as the wires spark
    and short,
and it's him when I won't talk
for days after an argument,
his small fists pounding the dust
    from the bag in the barn,
left jab to get it moving,
right cocked to knock it out,
my old man drinking with my hand
    on the patio after,
his lips singing my songs till 2 A.M.
and every neighbor's light is off
but I'm still looking for more
    of something
like him those nights in Boney's Bar,
the red neon bull charging down
while he bought for the house
and came home with nothing,
    the two of us
sitting silent then at either end
of the table in that unheated flat
    on Olmstead Street,

our skin blue-cold as his heart-struck
    death within a few months,
neither willing to go get a coat,
trying not to blink, tapping our fingers,
    our feet,
waiting for the other one to start.

I CAN'T FORGET YOU.

spray-painted high on the overpass,
each letter a good foot long,
and I try to picture the writer
    hanging from a rope
between dusk and dawn,
the weight of his love swaying,
    making a trembling
N and G, his mind at work
    with the apostrophe—
    the grammar of loss—
and his resistance to hyperbole,
    no exclamation point
    but a period at the end
that shows a heart not given
    to exaggeration,
a heart that's direct with a no-
    fooling-around approach,
and I wonder if he tested the rope
before tying it to the only tree I can see
    that would bear any weight,
or if he didn't care about the free-
    fall of thirty or more feet
as he locked his wrist to form such
    straight T's,
and still managed, dangling, to flex
    for the C and G,
knowing as he did, I'm sure,
the lover would ride this way each day
until she found a way around—
a winding back road with trees

and roadside tiger lilies, maybe
a stream, a white house, white fence,
    a dog in the yard, miles
from this black-letter, open-book,
    in-your-face missing
that the rain or Turnpike road crew
    will soon enough wash off.

The Silent Archangels

When asked, in that third-grade class,
to recite the names of the *Magnificent
   Seven,*
I could only think of the *Seventh Heaven*
my father'd whispered those nights
   on Olmstead Street,
the one with gold bartops and women
   with gold-tipped breasts,
Everything gold, he promised
as he lifted the shimmering glass
   of beer to the light,
the wedding ring glinting
although the woman had long ago
walked off our brown porch,
Sister Ann Zita's voice bringing me back
   to the rustling seats
where I stood muttering *I don't know,
   I don't know,*

the same words I utter today,
my son more than four hundred miles away,
my father dead more than thirty years,
my heart shooting such pain this morning
   as I lay alone in bed
I thought I was in my last few seconds
   and finally asked myself
why I broke my brother's nose with a telephone,
why I left Lorraine naked on the Chevy's front seat,
why I keep drinking and spend every night watching TV,
the Seven Archangels come back now to hover around me,

four of their names, Uriel, Michael, Gabriel, Raguel
    on my unholy tongue,
their names popping out of my mouth as fast as I could say
    them
but leaving the other three lost in the mind's dark
with their lilies and swords, their flaming spheres,
their scalloped wings spread wide on my either side,
nine curves in each and in each of those,
thousands upon thousands of lidless eyes.

The Eternal Present of the Ancient Chinese Poems

In all these poems there's not one mention
    of a snapping turtle
like the one lumbering right now
    out of our pond,
a good forty pounds, I guess,
with a head the size of a baseball,
    a neck
at least six inches long that instantly
    retracts back into its shell
when I snap shut *Tu Fu's Selected Poems,*
a creature older than China itself
    plodding
past the red and yellow rowboat
    toward the cat's blue bowl
at the mouth of the dark garage,
    his pace slow, unhurried
even when the barn swallows dive
    and scatter,
even when the dog howls but does
    not leave the porch,
the turtle and me eye-to-eye now
as I lean in my hammock and feel
    my body on the verge
of being tossed to the ground,
trying not to drop the book where
Autumn River flows without end
even as the snapper digs his beak deep
into the bowl of tuna-flavored *Meow Mix*
with snaps and chomps that carry clearly
    as a monastery bell.

Cover Girl Sparkle

The green, brocaded dress, string
   of diamond chips,
the amethyst ring glittering
that summer evening in your backyard—
that's what I'd bury you in, I think,
   when an old friend calls
to say you've been dead for a week—
not that girdle I'd wrestled with
   the night of the prom,
and not the hard-cupped bra
with three impossible hooks in back,
and definitely not the French twist
   that was so hard to unpin—
streaked hair I watched you wind up again
   on top of your head
after we'd slid back into our clothes
   and were almost ready to go—
when you brushed that gold sparkle
   on your eyelids
beneath the humming streetlight
as huge snowflakes fell, some
   upward draft
   lifting them back into the dark,
   the two of us leaning into the dash
to watch them disappear, appear, disappear
   again
as we shivered on the broad front seat
   of that old black Plymouth
where you flickered and flashed
   whenever you blinked.

(for D.G.)

Flicking

After twelve manhattans
we thought he'd just pass out,
but instead found him flipping
    the lawn lights,
sending messages to the hill rising
    behind our house
that sent back messages of its own,
those erratic fireflies suddenly
    starting up
as he kept flicking the switch,
which made those of us who were
    somewhat sober
    look at each other
and then at the man whose brain
    was about to explode
within a matter of months,
not one word out of his mouth
about the sensitive skin or strict
    diet,
not one syllable about the hair
    dropping in clumps,
the nights he could not love,
just that standing alone in what
    was dark
while the rest of us gathered
    on the porch
to watch his fingers turning
the night on, off, on, on, on.

(for J.M.)

Receiving at the Kneeling Rail

He stuck to my palate, unwilling
    to go down—
lodged at the top of my dirty throat
where I could use only my tongue
    to work His dryness off
as I knelt at the rail ordering my sins
    from least to worst,
trying to figure the one that was making
    me choke—
Lorraine's legs spread wide on the backseat
    of the Buick,
the ten bucks lifted from the Cohoes Theater's
    ticket box,
the curse when my mother strutted off the porch—
my eyes lifted now and then to the six stone
    angels
standing guard about the gold tabernacle
    that was His temple,
the gold door swinging so easily on its three
    gold hinges
I did not hear a creak or groan,
just the rustling of wings in there and a silence
    that shone,
and me, all eyes and ears at that hard rail,
    trying to muster some spit,
    trying not to let on.

The Disappearing Trick

You've vanished again, somehow
moved from the seventeenth row,
thirteenth stone in from the road,
snow flakes blown horizontal
across the wide sweep of the dead
while I stumble in cold feet,
cold hands hanging onto the plastic wreath
I intend to clamp to your grave
and tie secure with the thin green threads,
but you're nowhere to be found, gone,
just as you'd drifted out that back door
on Olmstead Street into twenty below,
jacket open, no hat, no gloves,
only khaki pants and white socks
glimmering above cheap boots
that let any weather in,
only the house of cards left trembling
    on the kitchen table
beneath that dim moon of a bulb,
the star-speckled linoleum gleaming
as it creaked, me turning in a circle
as though you were hiding behind me—
expecting the sudden tap on the shoulder,
the sudden hand-brush through my hair—
not believing anyone with such rings and keys
    and jangling coins
could so quickly, so silently, disappear.

Pear Tart

The mother called every day
    for a week
to ask this or that
for her son who was dying
    of leukemia
just discovered last month—
my wife the triage nurse
    with a soft voice
that said *Yes, just tell us*
    what you need,
we can send someone—

    till that night we sat
on the patio of Wassergass
eating crab cakes and sliced
    tomatoes
fresh from the garden,
our glasses brimmed
    with Merlot
that shimmered and reflected
    the sun-setting sky
where first the barn swallows
    and then the bats
    cut their zigzag paths,
when the telephone did not ring

and we munched little squares
of the tart made with homegrown
    pears
we'd scooped the bees from,
their wings so sticky with sweetness
they plummeted to the ground
where the birds came to peck at them.

II

Pitching in the Aggie

He'd close one eye and squint the other,
    lean his cheek to the alley dirt,
    then rise and consider
    the light, the wind
    before doing it all again,

the marble balanced, snug, between
    forefinger and thumb,
    glinting its cat's-eye
as he feinted, then pulled back
in a sun that shone brilliant

on old man Tremblay's three blue work
    shirts and darker blue pants,
the white gutter and downspout,
    the black bicycle's spokes,
    even my brother's fingernail,

the one he finally set to the earth and flicked
to pitch yet another aggie into the scooped hole,
    the click of it
rippling out that split-second to here,
where I sit, sixteen years after his death,

    watching it roll in.

(for N.R.)

A Room for Jesus

Each of us has a room inside
    for Jesus,
        Sister Aquinas hissed
during that heavenly blue
    catechism lesson
as she drew the castle with turrets
her faith had built, block by block,
curlicues of smoke rising from
    three chimneys
for the Father, Son, and Holy Ghost,
and a door that was never locked
so any sinner could just drop in,
Sister telling us to close our eyes
    and rap three times
    on our desks,
and when we opened them
we'd be inside with Jesus Himself,

    which I try years later,
after abortion, divorce, so many lies
    and thefts
I've stopped trying to count them up
    out here on the pond
in a rowboat with a sprung oarlock bolt,
    mosquitoes big as bees
buzzing every inch of my body
as I row with one oar in circles
that grow smaller and smaller until
    I'm dead in the center
of a pond so mucked I'm betting
    I'll never get out,

looking around for the door
　　Sister had drawn
back in that fifth-grade class,
　　the gold knob
she had sketched in yellow chalk,
my hand turning the air right, then left,
　　then right again,
　　listening for the slightest click
as the spring peepers wildly start up.

The Right Dress

My mother's voice cracks
over the phone as she lists
the things wrong with her back,
stomach, breasts, legs, and *God knows*
    what else,
she whispers when the litany's done,
closer to death than she's ever been,
and I'm worried how I will find
the crinoline dress she wants to be buried in,
    all those clothes pressed
in her closet like back on Olmstead Street,
    so tight she had to pry
one out to hold it to her body
    in front of the mirror,
do that half-turn right, then left before
    cramming it in again,
then another and another and another
while I was made to watch and judge
which one made her look thinner,
which one looked good with her color—
    black mascara on her lashes,
    teal shadow on her lids—
her eyes meeting my eyes beneath
    the dim bulb
only when she was getting ready
    to leave,
closer then than she'd ever been,
whispering in a voice so sweet
I'd repeat whatever she said
for hours after she'd left.

The starlings fill the trees

until they *are* the trees,
squeaks and squawks and screeches
weighting branches with blackness
lined glossy feather to feather
until, as though with one thought,
they all rise and figure eight, curve
four, five hundred feet to settle
on the black walnuts farther up the hill,
there, where we'd walk at dusk, her
always stopping to check her pulse,
catch her breath while I circled up and back,
tried to keep the little rhythm we'd started out with,
not wanting to lose the cardio benefit
although it was hard to walk away
only to turn and see her so small on the slope,
hear her counting in a whisper
that grew louder and louder the closer I got.

At the Breakfast Table with My
Seventeen-Year-Old Son

This, worse than his dentist visit,
sitting at the morning table with
    the coffee cups steaming,
my mouth filled with words,
his eyes stuck to the tablecloth,
    nothing wrong,
    no late-night driving
    to complain about,
    no overgrown grass or
    forgotten chores,
    no notes from school,
just this father-son, eye-to-eye
    at the breakfast table
where I ask how his car is running,
    how work is,
    his girl,
    will he be driving to the shore,
    will he be driving,
    will he
until he's driven the words out of me
    without a single word,
silence thicker than the coffee he'd made
    just minutes before,
humming some tune, singing some song,
what had brought me, hopeful, down the stairs
    before he was out the door,
where he stands now, hand fisted on the knob,
    back turned,
his muttered *so long* echoing, thundering
    my *so long.*

Car on the Road, Late July, Wassergass

It's the bass beat I hear first
as the car passes Yenni's house and
    starts to take the curve,
its drumming deeper than the German
    Shepherd's barking
and the rumbling of my neighbor's old
    John Deere tractor,
the glimpse I catch shiny, the driver's
    elbow out, jaunty,
as the song comes clear for an instant
    and then as suddenly fades
    past Carl's and Kelly's posted fence,
leaving me here in my orange and yellow
    hammock
with my finger on a line of Wang Wei's
    "Whirling Geisha,"
the old man out of breath just watching
    her dance
as I try to remember the name of the girl
    with short blond hair
who always leaned into me wherever
    we rode in the two-toned
blue and turquoise 1962 Plymouth,
the one who loved to fuck on the front
    seat, not the back,
who was thin and agile enough to move
    between me and the dash
    as these willow branches move,
    swaying right when I sway left,
    and left when I sway right,
my eyes now and then catching a glimpse
of her breasts in the clouds beyond the page.

Letter to HC in the Hospital

Mid-May here in Wassergass and more
birds than even you could name,
bird book splayed on the patio table
those mornings you sat in the frayed
    Black Watch bathrobe
smoking and drinking white cup after cup
    of coffee,
sometimes limping up to where I worked
    on the woodpile or stone row,
Magic, our dog, running beside you—
before your wife got the M.S.,
before your daughter died of the cancer,
before you started lugging that Oxy-Pac
from room to room where, I hear,
you sit down and don't want to stand back up,
like Magic those last few months,
    no longer making the stairs,
shitting everywhere, down to forty pounds,
    so we put him to sleep—
two seconds after the shot he was gone,
    head dropped sudden as a rock
    onto the vet's linoleum floor,
the kind with gold specks that are supposed
    to look like stars,
all that glittering around his black snout,
the eyes wide, still unafraid, still staring out
the way they would when he'd first spot
    a groundhog,
that split-second and he was off. Once
    we timed him, remember?—

seven seconds to cover the hundred feet
to the top of the hill and young walnuts,
    his teeth sinking in, one snap
    of the neck, all of it over in a flash,
and your brown-spotted hand, trembling,
coming down hard, pounding, on the timer
    of the clock.

MISSING

They're still hanging her picture
   by the fruit bins,
     glaring
among the bananas and kiwis,
the too-orange oranges
and five different kinds
   of apples—
   face thin,
the jaw dragged down
   even at ten,
the long hair stringy
on either side of cheeks
   that seem sucked in,
     eyes
full and glazed like yours
those last days we shopped here,
   you leaning on the green cart
as we roved from Cheetos to Crest
   to Ragu and last,
the Freihofer's apple turnovers you
   set on top
so they would not be crushed,
the ones you'd flake apart
   on the blue plate
when we got home, nibble at
   the sweetness
till you were done and left
   most of it lying there,
declaring you were stuffed,
your long blond hair so much
   like this missing child's

I have to stop and stare while
    carts rattle
and hues of hands reach into
    the cold light of bins
for a red, an orange, a gleaming
    green, a yellow,
remembering your instructions
    on how to press,
feel the heft, to listen hard
    when the watermelon
echoed your three short knocks.

(for D.R.)

Fireflies at the Cohoes Drive-In

While you watched Sean Connery jujitsu
    four men and roar away
    in a silver-gray Porsche
I was staring out at fireflies in the Cohoes Drive-In's
    erratic dark—
last row, nearly the last car all the way to the right
where the trees hung branches
        over the fence
and the fireflies rose and fell in a pattern
    I kept trying to make out despite
    the screen's glow
and the occasional car starting up to go—
parking lights on, red brake lights
    now and then down
    the dusty aisle,
an argument, maybe, or one had to get home,
or they'd already finger-fucked or blown
    or gone the whole way
and had climbed back into their wrinkled clothes
    to find the movie boring, the talk,
    the popcorn stale, soda flat,
    mosquitoes banging on the
    heated windows—

the fireflies flashing while I slipped
    off your black bra and black panties
    and you unzipped my jeans and
    took me in your gold-speckled
        lips,
leaving gleaming flecks on my penis long after you'd
    dressed

and walked to the concession stand for something
      suddenly craved,
Snowcaps, Jujube fruits, those thin hamburgers
      smothered with relish,
while I slumped in the front seat watching the light
      glint from my dick
with quick signals the fireflies kept flickering back.

The saints always

        had their hands up
with a cupped world, a rosary, a quill,
    a sword,
God's finger pointing at Adam and Eve,
at the snake, at me as I sat, slouched,
    in the last
seat of that fifth-grade class
    memorizing the Commandments,
    the Seven Deadly Sins,
    the Apostles' names,
picking out the one that fit me best,
    Thou Shalt Not Kill,
    Lust,
    Judas,
finding myself wherever I looked—
the bad thief hanging on his left-side cross,
    the snake
wound through an apple tree's branches
    twisted like the limbs I'd climb
    that dusk,
the one who clubbed his brother to death,
who threw his brother in a pit,
who ran away and spent his last cent,
who had the devil cast out of his house
only to have him return seven times worse again,
    Peter, gutless, denying Christ,
me knowing I was adopted no matter what
    they said—
the black angel there in my heart, my balls, my brain,
    wings spread wide,

carrying me off even as I chewed warts on my hands
    and sucked the blood
because I was afraid to let it drop on the desk
where I had carved tits and cunts and *shit*
    and *fuck,*
marks of sin Sister was sure to see
no matter how many beads of the rosary
    I prayed,
no matter how many correct answers I gave.

Card Game

Too dark to read, the book
closed, I think you are ten
years younger than your son,
silent up there on the windblown
bare hill of upstate New York
as you ever were at the kitchen table,
your bread route ledger snapped shut,
coins piled in columns soon to be swept
    into the breadman's purse,
before the glasses of beer and signals of smoke,
the jungle rot holes in your face
that slowly swallowed you up,
scene I keep coming back to
as though looking for a clue to who
    you were, who I was,
the two of us playing cards,
rummy, blackjack, stud poker
all night long without a word,
glad her sleeping pill worked,
glad the butcher knife was in the drawer,
the slap, slap, slap of cards
steady as the pulse in your neck
as you shuffled, and cut, and dealt.

III

Indulgences for the Dead

Each tug on the oar lifts my old man
    another inch out of the flames,
and I let the mosquito bite my foot
    twice
for the last seven drunken years
    of his life.
The horseflies take what they want
    from my arm, my thigh—
for his silence when she lifted
    the belt and swung
    and he did nothing
but blow those slow circles of blue
    smoke
into the yellow tin ceiling.
My whole back such an ache now
I know I will have trouble getting out
    of the boat—
those groans for his Friday nights
    at Boney's Bar
    buying drinks for the house
and coming home with third-day
    special raisin-bread loaves.
And this weed-slaked slime crusting
    on my hands
that I will not wash off till dusk—
for that Sunday morning I found him
    drunk
in the open-roofed blue Cadillac
    with four of his buddies, all
snoring in the sun of St. John's Alley
    while the church bells pealed,

his pock-marked face relaxed enough
    to show the two gold teeth
    glinting
like the diamond chip on his black
    onyx ring
that glittered from his tight-fisted grip
on the white velour steering wheel.

In the Expert Valet Clothing Shop

He's here, too, pock-marked skin,
beer breath, knees crossed,
thread between his teeth,
the silver needle gleaming
as he pushes in, pulls through,

this time in the guise
of a tailor from Portugal
who works in the Expert
Valet Clothing Shop
on Fourth Street, Bethlehem,

tiny, dapper man who looks up
with my old man's red eyes,
who moves with my old man's
birdlike arms and legs, that
quick, angled twist of neck

when he takes a sport coat
down from the rack
with the same brown hands,
smoothes the fabric as though
he were patting my hair

back on Olmstead Street
after his wife had left,
one son's madness,
the other son's death,
the Portuguese tailor

and my father both sad
as I shake my head
to the fine alpaca, the worsted

wool and combed cashmere,
the two of them holding my arm

as I start to leave, pulling
on my sleeve as they reach
for yet another coat on the rack,
asking me to wait just one more minute
so they can show me what else they have.

Another Lent, the purple shrouds

on saints, the thick incense,
and I remember what I tried to give up,
    what not,
chewing gum, candy, popcorn easy,
but lovely Lorraine's minted tongue,
lovely Lorraine's gold-sparkled lips
    and black silk bra
    so hard
I had to give them up again and again,
    as I do this morning,
listening to a country singer on a static
    station
belt out *Please Love Me Forever*
    and I do, I don't, I do,
    nodding and swaying
    in both places at once
as I ride down Wassergass Road,
seeing the inch-high cardinal tattooed
    above Lorraine's left nipple
more clearly now than any real cardinal,
flame-red feathers, flame-yellow beak,
its wings spread wide as my thumb
I press hard against the steering wheel
    to feel its pulse.

Trying to Read Han Shan

Han Shan never mentions a daughter
when he sits zazen, staring at Cold Mountain,
    the mountain staring back—
and certainly no Hendrix whammed on an ebony
        six-string Stratocaster
or set of drums rumbling "Stairway to Heaven."
And when he has his meal of rice and wine
there are no mounds of bras and skirts and pastel blouses
    thrown on the kitchen floor,
no pantry emptied of every Devil Dog and Oreo.
I see him taking long walks beside mossed rocks—
no teenage boyfriend speeding into his driveway,
    nearly killing the cats
that scatter faster than fallen yellow leaves
    in the sudden autumn wind,
and no sixteen-year-old daughter whispering she *needs*
three hundred dollars for her prom dress,
    and condoms *and* pills
because she's finally met the right guy—
Han Shan not hearing one of her words rising above
    the treble beat of her new love's
eight-speaker stereo that blasts, "You've got what I want
    and I want it bad,"
the old, broke poet climbing into his frail bark
even as I dog-ear the page and reach for my wallet,
    listening between the *boom boom boom*
    and her *please, please, please,*
    to the dip of his paddle

into the River of Ten Thousand Sorrows
that flows across the top of the page
where my daughter's glossy-black fingernails
    with silver stars
are tapping, tapping, and will not go away.

Limbo, Wassergass

It was always dark, and the souls had little wings
so they could fly but were mostly whirled
   in a wind they could not feel—
all the unbaptized African and Chinese kids
   swerving in and out
until God would come to judge them at the end of the world,
Sister Benedictus hissed in that fourth-grade class,
her words still clear through these fifty years
as I listen to the news about another Baghdad bombing,
God's lightning in a barrage of missiles,
God's Word another inarticulate string of sentences
   about the Unbelievers, the Infidels,
as the camera zooms in on the armless boy
with flies clustering on his bandaged stumps,
and on the mother screaming into the lens
that her daughter has been buried for three days now
   beneath the rubble of her exploded house,
the whirling of wings even here in Wassergass
where I'm figuring our distance from Washington,
   Philadelphia, New York,
the fastest route out when the bomb finally goes off,
how far we'd have to get to be beyond the parameter of fallout,
the clouds now gathering overhead real clouds,
with real lightning that's striking just over South Mountain,
   and thunder that shakes the house,
my wife calling me to the porch where we watch hundreds
of birds rise from the evergreens to circle and whirl
   in the glowing, electrified air—
making those high cries no one in his right mind could mistake for song.

Poison Sumac

I could go for a walk again, up there along the stone rows
    loaded with poison sumac,
I could commit my little act against the gods of reason
    once again
by bending down their poisonous heads, prying out one
    red poisonous seed at a time—
like this one, the one I will call brother,
give that long black hair with a wave vaselined into place forever,
and the black onyx ring with a diamond chip and a gold initial,
    that lone *N*,
and even the last parachute jump from 30,000 feet, that fall
    in which his mind left,
and one for the hundreds of electro-shocks,
and one for the kisses from women who slept with his madness,
    bless them,
and here, another seed for that afternoon he took me and my brother
    to the movies with the dollar he'd earned on the milk route,
and here, one for the peanut butter jar he hid behind his ass
that he scooped a big chunk from with his forefinger
and then smacked and smacked his lips as he swallowed it,
and of course one for his years of two-inch, thorazined steps,
    a big, ripe, red one for that,
and one for his three packs of Camels a day despite the emphysema
    and cancer and weakening heart, a dried, browning one for that,
and here, in the center of the pod, the point from which all of the seeds radiate,
here, the one for the three nameless men in the VA Hospital who held him down
    in the shower and fucked him in the ass
while the water ran hot, then cold as ice, then hot again, the way my brother
    remembered it,
the center seed for that, the one hard to pry out, the one that, when lifted up,
    leaves that soft, startling white spot.

Lucky

First it was three
pink rabbits' feet
hanging from a key chain,
then three knocks on wood,
how he'd rap my head
if there were none around,
then the three bottles of beer,
girlfriends, pillows, sons,
once even cars, sure
the third was always the best,
the one that would last,
why he said in the will
to plant him in this field
of St. Joseph's Cemetery
between his first and third sons,
all three cars in the dump
for scrap before he was
set into the ground,

cold and dark as that night
    at Saratoga
when he spent the rent money
on a definite hunch,
tearing the tickets and throwing
them on the heads below us
until three guys came up,
my father ready to fight them all,
raising his fists, swearing,
making the sign of the cross
just before he swung and missed,
finding himself behind bars

while I stood and talked,
his bony finger shaking
at me most of the night,
the middle, busted one
he'd tell the weather with
when he and my mother used to sit
on the brown porch, holding it
up like a lightning rod
to the gathering clouds.

Suet

Her smudged red lips,
her smudged black lids,
and I am following her to the stove
where she is frying livers and onions
    in thick suet I will soon eat,
my mother mad as she clicks the gas,
the flame not low, not high enough
as she curses my father and the snow
of that upstate New York winter falling
    faster, thicker,
as though to bury the two of us together,
me watching as she slides it all from the pan,
then scrapes the mound of suet on top,
telling me it will make my hair curly, not
    so straight,
that it will make my bones strong, not so
    weak,
that it will help me to talk, get rid of my
    stutter, my mother
bending to whisper, *Enjoy your life now,*
    it won't get any better,
the blue veins of her hands bulging as she grips
    the chair
and sits to make sure I clean my plate.

Bullfrog, Wassergass

One of the bullfrogs is so out of pitch
    even our drunk friend
stops his twirling patio dance
to mutter, "You fuckin' hear that?",
the rest of us nodding, looking up
as though it would help us to hear
    what he was talking about,
the black spots on the rim of the night
    pond
growing darker with each odd note,
    each off-beat croak,
all of us knowing our friend's voice
would soon enough crack like that,
the hole, the box in the throat, the old
    story
of a matter of weeks, maybe months,
but for now there was just the clinking
    of drinks and that one frog
off to the southwest berm of the pond,
the one we followed for a good half-hour
    by flashlight but never found,
his erratic call rising in the dark from where
    we thought he was but wasn't,
and our friend, calling back, pointing,
    stumbling
till he got stuck, ankle deep, in the shallow
    muck,
refusing to lift a hand to help us pull him out.

Sequence

My son out in the dark
   picking the last
   tomatoes and peppers
he's weeded and mulched
   and watered all summer,
the night of the first frost
   here,
the TV announcer almost
   shouted,

so he went out with the
   flashlight
I watched him tuck
in his jacket pocket
   to pick his crop,

and I wanted to ask if
   I could help,
I wanted to say I could
   hold the light.
I wanted to say I should
never have let him ride
   his bike
seventeen years ago
on Wassergass Road
where the heavy Buick
sent him flying over
   a hundred feet,

his atrophied leg, his right
   eye lower than the left,
his inability to sequence

more than three steps
    at a time—

steps to write an essay,
steps for three time blocks
before and after lunch,
steps to solve for X—

but I kept quiet, sat flicking
    the remote control
while the door clicked
and his light zigzagged

    up the black
till he got to the gate—
    lifting the latch
while holding the flashlight,
    wavering,
under his chin or in his mouth,

and third, the easy swinging out.

Sleep-Eaze

I don't even hear the geese
honking as they dive-bomb the pond
    on March 5 A.M.'s,
and I don't hear our son's
    alarm,
the clump of his boots
down the creaking stairs,
nor the telephone ringing
    in the living room
where you used to stay up
    talking
because you could not sleep,
when I feigned tiredness
and went to bed to turn
your Christmas gift, *Sleep-Eaze,*
    up to ten
on Waterfall with overlay of Frogs
    and Doves,
or Forest with Soaring Owls,
but usually on Surf with Train,
that chug-chug so oddly comforting
    as I was on my way
down tracks that dully gleamed
like those when I was twelve
    or thirteen
and would run along the Cohoes
    Freight,
leaping for the iron bar to swing
    up and in
for the ride to Albany, no fear
of the clickety-clacking wheels

that somehow shone even when
    there was no sun,
no fear of falling off to cinder
    and glass,
or wondering if anyone would be
    home when I returned,
traveling mile after mile
    for no reason at all
except to get somewhere and then
    turn back.

IV

The Chasm

Our daughter feels for her pulse
first on her neck and then her wrist,
a trick she learned from her mother
those nights she could not catch
    her breath,
and she does it again here
    in the doctor's office
where we have come to talk about
    Risperdal and Zoloft,
her sixteen years of drifting toward
the corners of rooms and playgrounds,
how she does not dare sit in a front desk
    of any class and raise her hand.
Our daughter has started to bite past
    her fingernails into flesh,
    drawing blood.
She's begun to daydream while
    she talks, losing
the ends of sentences to what
the doctor calls a deep chasm.
Picture her there, he murmurs,
    motioning us close
when our daughter excuses herself
    to go to the bathroom,
the three of us leaning from our
    chairs,
bowing our heads, nodding
at the industrial-brown carpet.

Four-Way Switch

My father could not hammer a nail straight
    or level a shelf,
he could not open a summer-stuck window;
the one time he tried to fix the kitchen light,
sparks flew like fireworks on the Fourth of July—
and so I find myself out here on a ladder for days
replacing clapboard and aligning gutter,
cracking concrete and priming boards for trim,
making the miter cuts exact so I will not need caulk,
now and then telling my long-dead father
Look, it's this easy, or *See, this is how it's done,*
whispering as he did those last seven years after
    she'd left,
my voice growing more and more like his
    till it's 9 P.M.
    and we've been out here 14 hours,
wiring the last outlets and the four-way switch,
the one that will light from the entrance,
    bottom of stairs, and again at the top,
the one that would have burnt my father up,
    toasted him if he'd attempted it,
the one I cannot stop clicking in the dark,
    the light, the dark.

The Ninth Circle, Wassergass

Pewter snow, no sun, five below,
this surely the Ninth Circle of Hell
Sister Thomas had hissed about back
    in that sixth-grade class,
making us count off the nine days
the Black Angels fell into the abyss
where God cast the whores and drunks,
my mother falling from God's list, I knew,
    father, too,
and me, for looking up Ann Harding's
    plaid skirt,
for carving *Fuck* in the etched
    lopsided heart on the desk,

landing here in Pennsylvania Wassergass
where my dick goes limp in my wife's
    mouth
and the three herniated disks throb
    and throb,
where the MRI shows spinal stenosis,
and the doctor says soon enough
    a replaced hip,
knowing I'm on the rack that Sister
    had promised for all us sinners,

the one she drew on the board in red chalk
    with little wheels and a toothed bar
that stretched the sinner's bones till they broke,
telling us the muscles would never knit,
the skin tear and crack and never mend,
as she grasped the rack's handle of air
and ratcheted it ten times before Al Audon's

desk for the wine he'd sipped after mass,
ten more beside Ann Harding's for the short
    skirt, the gold sparkle on her lips,

Sister wafting her black-robed way down
    the aisle toward where I sat
with hands folded and both feet on the floor,
looking straight ahead at Irene Legasse
    who I'd felt up in the clothes closet,
at Richie Freeman who I'd slapped in the head
    at recess,
my mind racing with all the sins I'd committed
even as she lifted the opened hand and curled
    her fingers slowly into a fist
that pushed forward and pulled back—
    fifteen, twenty, twenty-five—
telling me she knew I knew what I had done
even as she made that click-click-click
    with the tip of her pink tongue.

I keep repeating the name of the concerto

just as I repeat the names of the flowers she kept
    pointing to
while the music wafted out the screened window,
the garden now just a rectangle of mulch
    with a few sodden stalks
when I walk past it to the field, the slight hill and woods
    beyond,
the tune of the concerto in our bodies back then as we walked,
    our fingers moving to it,
    our hands up and waving to it,
slow, at times, with an oboe or flute—when she'd stop
    to catch her breath,
    and then fast—a clarinet, a trumpet—
when she'd say ok and we'd keep up a good pace
    for another few hundred feet,
by then the concerto way behind us, unheard as it filled
    the empty rooms of our white house,
the two of us in a rhythm that was the concerto's rhythm,
carrying us through the field of white pine and spruce,
    past the quarry and around the pond,
the rhythm we'd walk back down the hill to—sometimes
    taking bets on who would hear it first,
    that one the winner,
who could be the conductor, waving the imaginary baton,
telling the other to get in step, or how beautiful
    their playing was,
the two of us nodding our heads, strumming
    or plunking or banging keys,
or on the boldest days, breaking into song.

Letter #3 to Carruth about the Heron

He's come back, bigger
    than ever,
wingspan a good six feet,
    longer than you

stretched out in that hospital bed
    friends tell me about,

second bout of pneumonia
after the quadruple bypass
and all those New Age doctors
    sizing you up

as you mumbled about
    the Christs
tacked to the trees on the hill
    behind your house,

old man who talked to Ovid
    and Tu Fu,

although you had no idea
    how to jack up
the joists to replace your rotted
    sill
that last afternoon I came to visit,

our two heads bent in the
    low cellar
as I said *pole jack,*
    2 x 6 scabs
    to take the weight,

and you, one of the few times,
    listening,

following my finger
as I pointed here, there,
leaned close to shout

Just an inch a day
or it will all come down

into your good ear.

Hanging Tinsel

The two of us in that dark room
where the only lights were blinking bulbs
with liquid that boiled to the tops
    and settled down all night long
while you set single silver thread after thread
    until the needled branch gleamed
    and you moved on,
left me beside the three reindeer tugging
    the five-inch plywood slat-sled
    she'd left,
your slender fingers doling out those silver
    strings,
lifting and setting each separate, glittering
    strand
until there were waves of silver wafting
    whenever one of us shifted or bent,
    whole walls of shimmerings
that reflected us back in thin strips,
your ringed hand, my left shoulder,
    your nose, my eyebrow, shreds
    of us hung on those branches
    sagged
with candy canes and red-eyed, scraggly-feathered
    white birds,
with snow-painted pinwheels that whirled
    in our slightest whisper,
your white sweatshirt there, a sliver
    of your khaki pants,

the right side of my mouth, my ear,
there in the stillness of our held breaths
    as we stretched out to hang yet
    another, and another, and another
    silver thread.

Snowflakes in Hell

We would all melt from the heat
    of our sins
like snowflakes in Hell,
Sister Benedictus croaked
as we traced and cut flakes
from the heavy, white construction
    paper,
such odd angles sprinkled with silver
    sparkle
I find myself even now tilting
to make some sense of them,

seeing again those flakes I've held, palm up,
    in gloved hands,
those I've watched float on fur collars
where my warm breath melted them
as I leaned down for this kiss, that kiss,
flakes slapped against the windshield
    to instantly melt
on those many-miled treks
to the Albany V.A. Hospital
for brother in his electro-shocked
    cell,
my first love blowing me in the great
    snowstorm of that year
when the radio warned they could not clear
    the Interstate,
but we would not stop or turn around
while those silver flakes fell, glittering

like that sparkle flung with a quick twist
    of our nine-year-old wrists

onto the six triangle tips that formed
even as red and yellow Hell flames roared
on the blackboard of that fourth-grade class,
Sister shouting that the very heat of our bodies
    was Satan's work
before she asked for a show of hands of who
    was cold, who was not,
the seven sinners made to clear our desks
    and move to the farthest row
against the windows where those flakes
    we'd struggled to make
    neither rose nor fell,
just floated there in such erratic shapes,
    taped to what was clearly invisible.

Considering Aunt Bea's white Toyota Celica

that day she roared into the driveway
    in the low-slung,
    muffler-growling,
    red-leather-seated,
    eight-speaker-stereo-blasting
    brand-new convertible,
when she could not stop flipping
the halogen headlights on and off,
    insisting I get in and drive,
her ring-studded hand on my hand to guide
    me through the two extra gears
once we got to the straight-away on Wassergass Drive—
    up to eighty-five
when she looked me in the face
and said it could take a lot more than that,
    the two of us shifting the stick
as she whispered with those hot-pink lips
    for me to ease up on the clutch,
    take her for a *real* ride.

(for B.A.)

Right after Mass

Plastic crucifixes glinted
from my grandmother's rusted fence
as she bent to twist white bandages
    around limp tomato plants,
lay the mulch with a *Satan begone,*
her flick of wrist the same as at high mass
    when she splattered holy water
on our young faces that watched her pass,
    the priest's helper, God's aid
who'd cross herself all the way
up Ontario and down Olmstead
    until she could kneel
in the chrism-blessed dirt of her own backyard
to tap in the seeds with the Holy Spirit
    still upon her,
arms spread wide in that morning light
    as I balanced on the fence
to watch her separate the good from the bad,
    The wheat from the chaff
    as she'd whisper it,
reminding me my mother would still be
    sleeping it off,
that my father's piss-stained sheets hung
    like flags of sin just four yards down,
telling me as she rose on dirt-crusted knees
    that I, too, would be turned
into a swine and driven off some high cliff
    if I did not heed the mark
    God had branded me with,

her thick hands grasping the splotched shape
    of purple wings
stretched across the back of my neck
that even then were lifting me up.

Inside the dim kitchen the rosary

was making the rounds,
the circle of old women in flower-
   print dresses
bending their heads and uttering

while I waited on the porch
   wishing I smoked,
wishing I could put my fist through
   the brick wall,

feeling my father's death rising in me,
and my mother's last walk off the porch,
telling myself to just stand absolutely
   still

in that upstate New York
   early November cold,
watching sleet-rain silver
the few leaves left on the maple,

the ones I started to count, then stopped,
   then started again, knowing
   it'd take a long, long time
and there was no way I'd ever get it right.

Window Candle

The bulb flickers on so easily,
with a millimeter twist, lit
so my long-dead father might see
I have not forgotten him on this
thirtieth Christmas of his death,
knowing he is somewhere out there,
maybe as far north as upstate New York
or closer, by those norway maples
on the far side of the pond,
hands still in his chinos,
white sweatshirt, no coat
although it's six below,
the two of us knowing
he could be like that all night long,
No piss in the blood, as he'd joke
those dawns we shoveled three-, four-,
five-foot drifts of snow
for the entire block, steam
whistling from our lips,
never a word between us,
like today, as I twist the bulb
till it glows and I see again
I have his fingers, his hands,
the short lifeline that instantly flares up.

V

Heaven's Gate

Only Gabriella Wells or Irene Duval
in their white dresses and tight curls,
maybe Al Bouchard in his pressed
pants and starched white shirt
might get through *Heaven's Gate*
that Sister Maria had drawn on the board,
the gold bars in yellow chalk,
the silver keys in white chalk,
where Michael, the huge archangel
with three heads, six faces,
twelve wings and a sword stood guard
and would not let anyone in
who had the slightest sin
    on his soul,

those of us placed in the last row
sure we were going to Hell,
Donald, who'd been held back two years,
Richie, who smoked and cursed,
Jon DuMas, who could not speak English,
and so drew the whole day long—
crosses filling the white page,
with devils rising from each one,
horns, pitchforks, penises
that dragged along the ground—

and me there, too, for the thirteen U's
of unsatisfactory moral behavior,
    a perfect score
my father joked when I brought
    the report card home,
the long ball, he whispered,

so the woman at the stove would not hear,
bending so close I could smell the Schaefers,
    see the quick signature
before he tucked it into my religion book
    whose cover I still remember,
a snow-capped mountain where tiny figures
    were climbing into a vast, blue cold,
each one with a red hat and a red scarf on,
all of them staring up, not one looking back
as they trudged, step by slow step, toward
    the smiling face of God.

Our Son Leaves His Miniature Japanese Sand Garden Behind Because There Will Be No Room in the Dorm

His bamboo rake is two inches long,
    with four prongs
that, when I lift them from the sand,
have left what look like his tooth marks
on my arm when he was what?, one?,
    one-and-a-half?,
his teeth cutting through the gums
making him howl and chomp down hard,
and I let him, felt the budding
    teeth sink in,
settle, till he fell asleep here
    in this room where
the statue of Laughing Buddha
    sits cross-legged
beside the black enameled box
of sand that has two S-curves at top
    and bottom,
three black sharks' teeth dropped
    randomly, but not—
a triangle, an arched eyebrow,
    a winged roof, or
three people standing about
the same distance apart,
one's hand up and waving
    as he turns,
the other two wildly waving back.

Compensate

The pearl-gray sky darkens
till without knowing when it happened
   it's night
and you're still out here shoveling
as you were with your father, and his,
the three herniated discs nothing,
nor the spinal stenosis, the new pain
in the left shoulder that comes from compensating
   for the weakness of the right,
the word *compensate* what you roll in your mind
   for a good hour
while you talk with your long-dead father,
   back-and-forthing
about why his wife high-heeled off the porch,
your voices rising and falling with the wind
till you turn, soaking, back toward the house,
hat, boots, gloves, jacket tossed in the center of the floor
   where you watch the ice melt and know again
   you've been somewhere else,
and a part of you, a big part, is still there, listening
to what sounds like the sound of your voice.

The Failed Trick

The white mouse went first, pink eyes, pink feet,
then the ace of hearts, the quarter and half-dollar,
    the pigeon, the cat,
once the dog, who didn't howl for a good hour,
    wherever he was,
our old man's hands faster than our eyes
as we lined up on the picnic table seat
to watch him toss the black cape on whatever
    came into range,
once getting our mother under that dark,
her blue bathrobe and red lips, the pink rollers
sticking out at all angles with twirls of hair,
    while he waved his hands above her,
chanting words we'd never understand,
    and then the tap of the wand,
the side of the box flipped up, flipped down
    to show her still cowering,
looking at us to see if we could see her
under the clothesline sagged with underwear,
    socks, shirts, and pants
she would soon enough have to unclip and fold
    in the blue basket,
our mother touching her arms and legs to make sure
    she was all there,
uncoiling slowly in the sun with both feet on the ground,
where she walked around us without a word
before disappearing into the shadowed door of the house.

My Father, Setting the Line, Sunny October

The white string taut, the pitch set,
the sod sliced off and earth dug down
    four feet
so the frost would not heave it an inch,

and you, leaning your good eye along
    the earth to double-check
what two level bubbles had already
    checked,
waving that busted-knuckled finger
    of yours a hair to the left,
    back, there, that's right,

and me on the other end of the string
    that grew from your hand
the way I'd seen a spider spin a silk strand
    from yarrow stem to goldenrod,

    more of it coming the harder I pulled,

sun-struck and wind-swayed but not one
    sag
in what became the base line, the bottom line
    upon which our house was built.

Monitoring Impulses

The tube jiggles each time
   I swallow,
each time I breathe, so
I try not to eat,
I try to sip the air
so the monitor won't jolt
with its green alarm,
so it won't flash that
red exclamation point
straight at my heart,
electrical impulses
running up and down
my legs, my arms,
into my eyes where streaks
of light are no longer
angels or old lovers
but a fluorescent screen
green as the clock's hands
last night when I rolled
onto the empty side
of my sleep to find
you gone again, a list
forming that promised
to go on and on like this
jagged line blips
up and down with negative
and positive charges
packed tight in cells
that make me who I am,
a man in sweat pants and
   flannel shirt

sipping coffee as though
    I wasn't,
ready for the rush of wings
with the next bite of toast.

Sister Aquinas, Questioning

I wake to the dark the way
   I woke
to Sister Aquinas rapping
   on my desk
back in that fifth-grade class,
   asking
Where have you been?
What will you make of your life?—
the questions still ringing as I turn
   from side to side
to ease the pain in my back,
   my right leg,
hacking into the Kleenex set
on the bedside table each night,
trying to remember where my
   wife is,
what day, what season,
my mind racing for answers
as it did back then when Sister
floated down that narrow aisle,
   black robes out like wings
that wafted our small heads behind her
till she reached the blackboard and whirled
   to ask the nine names of God,
calling on me—the one who had fallen
   asleep, fallen behind,
the one who could not tell the difference
   between dark and light—
to stand and answer the question,
to pray if I didn't know, to search my soul
   as long as I needed to get it right.

Peaches in Pennsylvania Late August

For a week now I've been eating peaches,
letting the juices dribble down my chin,
I've been peeling and slicing and dicing them

for peach jam sealed tight with those
little lids where miniature peaches glow—
and for peach sorbet, peach cobbler, peach pie—

thinking how life is like this,
no peaches for fifty weeks and suddenly peaches
appear in baskets, blue bowls, on every imaginable plate,

opening my eyes just this morning to see two peaches
set side-by-side on the blue-fringed bedside table
where her 36C black bra and black silk panties gleamed

in a peach light as they heaved in and out of sight
with each rise and fall of her perfectly peach-shaped ass.

What does a man who's 55 say

when he sees his long-dead father
    walking over the rim
    of a frozen pond
    toward him,
ungloved hands up and waving,
no hat on his head, no scarf wrapped
    about the thin neck
although it's zero degrees and the
biggest storm of the year is swirling?
    It's been a long time.
    Where have you been?
And then there's the silence of you two
    walking side by side again,
not holding hands, no arms around shoulders
for you were never that kind of boy and man,
    but close enough so now and then
    your bodies would brush,
and you, the child, might stumble into his foot—
    but what, at that moment,
when what you've been thinking about
for more than half your life has finally happened,
    is the next word out of your mouth?,
     the next gesture?,
once you've reached for the knob on the door,
    given it that slight twist
    and asked him to enter?

Window of Our Soul

When Sister Sylvia told us to cut
    the window of our soul
on the thick construction paper
    and then lift it to peer in,
twenty-one second-graders sat
    at our desks
moving the squares of paper up,
    then down, and up again,
and I'd be lying if I told you that
    I saw nothing
but Ann Harding and Tommy Ryan
    two rows ahead—
that the window lifted only on the huge,
    wooden cross
and the still flag, or just the blackboard
    where nine planets
revolved around a black sun.
And I'd be foolish to tell you
    of the angel
whose wings grew on my either side,
whose light flowed from my eyes,
or of the quickness of my heart when I
    lifted up
to let what felt like a rush of cool air
    in—
and if I mention love and ascension,
or a lightness I have not felt
    in the past fifty years,
or the thought of joy, of streaming
right there and then through the opening
    into the mystery of the other side,

how could I even think of asking you
    to believe me,
since I did not go, since I stayed here
    with you instead.

Dinner with My Son, Casey Lynn's Diner, Hellertown

It was Alpo, I think, a big can
I opened one night to scoop
into the heavy frying pan
with gobs of ketchup,
stirring the five minutes it took
for the fat to form its own puddle
beneath the lump of lard I'd dropped in,
and it tasted good, like hash,
except there were more chunks of meat,
and it was cheap enough for me to eat
three meals of it a week,

that's what I'm thinking
as my son orders T-bone steak
with a double helping of mashed potatoes
at Casey Lynn's Diner, puts down the menu
and tells me about his hard day of numbers
and planets and musical scales.
His uniform tie pulled away from his neck,
the top button of the white shirt undone,
he is thirteen, about to enter the kingdom
of women who call him on his own phone
and whisper to his whisper
what he thinks no one knows.

It was 1966,
my father dead, my brother dying,
and I was a college kid living with the very rich Reynolds,
cutting their grass, splitting their wood, walking their
    dogs
in return for a room and a shower at the end of the
    servants' corridor.

Jimmy Charette had been shot in the head,
Glenn Brust about to have a mortar shell blow him apart
and I'd lie in the lumpy bed reading Milton, *nine days*
    they fell,
and Heidegger, whose thought-paths flashed on my eyelids
    whenever I pressed too tight.

I was getting ready for my first wife's death from bone
    cancer,
and my brother's onslaught of madness.
I was getting ready for my own heart to turn blacker
    than days-old blood,
ready for the lies to roll so easily from my tongue,
for the unforgiving mornings waking to the same sun.
I was getting ready for another can of dog food,
which wasn't so bad once I got past the stink,
the thick chunks giving me more red blood cells
and some extra fat to burn off those nights
I pored over the books that contained the secret of life,
all of it leading me here, a bit overweight, hair white,
able to put two twenties down with only a twinge of regret,
able to take the change without counting it up,
trying to forget the dessert my son ordered, half
of it left on the plate I have to tear my eyes from.

LEN ROBERTS is the author of nine books of poetry, the most recent being *The Disappearing Trick.* He has received numerous awards in poetry, including a Guggenheim Fellowship, two National Endowment for the Arts Poetry Awards, a National Endowment for the Humanities Translation Award, and six Pennsylvania Council on the Arts Poetry Awards. His fourth book, *Black Wings,* was selected by Sharon Olds for the National Poetry Series. His poetry also has been selected for The Best American Poetry and the Pushcart Prize.

In addition to his volumes of poetry, Roberts has had two chap-books and two books of his translations from the Hungarian published, including his most recent *Before and After the Fall: New Poems by Sandor Csoori.* He began his translation work while a Fulbright Scholar to Hungary; he was also a Fulbright Scholar to Finland and a Fulbright Translator to Hungary and Romania.

Other Books by Len Roberts

POETRY

The Silent Singer: New and Selected Poems (2001)
Lighting Up (chapbook, 2000)
The Trouble-Making Finch (1998)
Counting the Black Angels (1994)
The Million Branches (chapbook, 1993)
Dangerous Angels (1993)
Learning about the Heart (chapbook, 1991)
Black Wings (1989)
Sweet Ones (1988)
From the Dark (1984)
Cohoes Theater (1981)

TRANSLATIONS FROM THE HUNGARIAN

Before and After the Fall: New Poems by Sándor Csoóri (2004)
Waiting and Incurable Wounds (chapbook of Sándor Csoóri poems, 2000)
Selected Poems of Sándor Csoóri (1992)
Call to Me in My Mother Tongue (chapbook of Sándor Csoóri poems, 1990)

PROSE

To Write a Poem . . . (1994)

Illinois Poetry Series

Laurence Lieberman, Editor

Healing Song for the Inner Ear
Michael S. Harper (1984)

The Passion of the Right-Angled Man
T. R. Hummer (1984)

Dear John, Dear Coltrane
Michael S. Harper (1985)

Poems from the Sangamon
John Knoepfle (1985)

In It
Stephen Berg (1986)

The Ghosts of Who We Were
Phyllis Thompson (1986)

Moon in a Mason Jar
Robert Wrigley (1986)

Lower-Class Heresy
T. R. Hummer (1987)

Poems: New and Selected
Frederick Morgan (1987)

Furnace Harbor: A Rhapsody of the
North Country
Philip D. Church (1988)

Bad Girl, with Hawk
Nance Van Winckel (1988)

Blue Tango
Michael Van Walleghen (1989)

Eden
Dennis Schmitz (1989)

Waiting for Poppa at the Smithtown
Diner
Peter Serchuk (1990)

Great Blue
Brendan Galvin (1990)

What My Father Believed
Robert Wrigley (1991)

Something Grazes Our Hair
S. J. Marks (1991)

Walking the Blind Dog
G. E. Murray (1992)

The Sawdust War
Jim Barnes (1992)

The God of Indeterminacy
Sandra McPherson (1993)

Off-Season at the Edge of the World
Debora Greger (1994)

Counting the Black Angels
Len Roberts (1994)

Oblivion
Stephen Berg (1995)

To Us, All Flowers Are Roses
Lorna Goodison (1995)

Honorable Amendments
Michael S. Harper (1995)

Points of Departure
Miller Williams (1995)

Dance Script with Electric Ballerina
Alice Fulton (*reissue, 1996*)

To the Bone: New and Selected Poems
Sydney Lea (1996)

Floating on Solitude
Dave Smith (*3-volume reissue, 1996*)

Bruised Paradise
Kevin Stein (1996)

Walt Whitman Bathing
David Wagoner (1996)

Rough Cut
Thomas Swiss (1997)

Paris
Jim Barnes (1997)

The Ways We Touch
Miller Williams (1997)

The Rooster Mask
Henry Hart (1998)

The Trouble-Making Finch
Len Roberts (1998)

Grazing
Ira Sadoff (1998)

Turn Thanks
Lorna Goodison (1999)

Traveling Light:
Collected and New Poems
David Wagoner (1999)

Some Jazz a While:
Collected Poems
Miller Williams (1999)

The Iron City
John Bensko (2000)

Songlines in Michaeltree: New and
Collected Poems
Michael S. Harper (2000)

Pursuit of a Wound
Sydney Lea (2000)

The Pebble: Old and New Poems
Mairi MacInnes (2000)

Chance Ransom
Kevin Stein (2000)

House of Poured-Out Waters
Jane Mead (2001)

The Silent Singer: New and Selected
Poems
Len Roberts (2001)

The Salt Hour
J. P. White (2001)

Guide to the Blue Tongue
Virgil Suárez (2002)

The House of Song
David Wagoner (2002)

X =
Stephen Berg (2002)

Arts of a Cold Sun
G. E. Murray (2003)

Barter
Ira Sadoff (2003)

The Hollow Log Lounge
R. T. Smith (2003)

In the Black Window: New and
Selected Poems
Michael Van Walleghen (2004)

A Deed to the Light
Jeanne Murray Walker (2004)

Controlling the Silver
Lorna Goodison (2005)

Good Morning and Good Night
David Wagoner (2005)

American Ghost Roses
Kevin Stein (2005)

Battles and Lullabies
Richard Michelson (2005)

Visiting Picasso
Jim Barnes (2006)

The Disappearing Trick
Len Roberts (2006)

National Poetry Series

Eroding Witness
Nathaniel Mackey (1985)
Selected by Michael S. Harper

Palladium
Alice Fulton (1986)
Selected by Mark Strand

Cities in Motion
Sylvia Moss (1987)
Selected by Derek Walcott

The Hand of God and a Few
Bright Flowers
William Olsen (1988)
Selected by David Wagoner

The Great Bird of Love
Paul Zimmer (1989)
Selected by William Stafford

Stubborn
Roland Flint (1990)
Selected by Dave Smith

The Surface
Laura Mullen (1991)
Selected by C. K. Williams

The Dig
Lynn Emanuel (1992)
Selected by Gerald Stern

My Alexandria
Mark Doty (1993)
Selected by Philip Levine

The High Road to Taos
Martin Edmunds (1994)
Selected by Donald Hall

Theater of Animals
Samn Stockwell (1995)
Selected by Louise Glück

The Broken World
Marcus Cafagña (1996)
Selected by Yusef Komunyakaa

Nine Skies
A. V. Christie (1997)
Selected by Sandra McPherson

Lost Wax
Heather Ramsdell (1998)
Selected by James Tate

So Often the Pitcher Goes to Water
until It Breaks
Rigoberto González (1999)
Selected by Ai

Renunciation
Corey Marks (2000)
Selected by Philip Levine

Manderley
Rebecca Wolff (2001)
Selected by Robert Pinsky

Theory of Devolution
David Groff (2002)
Selected by Mark Doty

Rhythm and Booze
Julie Kane (2003)
Selected by Maxine Kumin

Shiva's Drum
Stephen Cramer (2004)
Selected by Grace Schulman

The Welcome
David Friedman (2005)
Selected by Stephen Dunn

Michelangelo's Seizure
Steve Gehrke (2006)
Selected by T. R. Hummer

Other Poetry Volumes

Local Men and *Domains*
James Whitehead (1987)

Her Soul beneath the Bone: Women's
Poetry on Breast Cancer
Edited by Leatrice Lifshitz (1988)

Days from a Dream Almanac
Dennis Tedlock (1990)

Working Classics: Poems on Industrial
Life
Edited by Peter Oresick and Nicholas Coles
(1990)

Hummers, Knucklers, and Slow Curves:
Contemporary Baseball Poems
Edited by Don Johnson (1991)

The Double Reckoning of Christopher
Columbus
Barbara Helfgott Hyett (1992)

Selected Poems
Jean Garrigue (1992)

New and Selected Poems, 1962–92
Laurence Lieberman (1993)

The Dig and *Hotel Fiesta*
Lynn Emanuel (1994)

For a Living: The Poetry of Work
Edited by Nicholas Coles and Peter Oresick
(1995)

The Tracks We Leave: Poems on
Endangered Wildlife of North America
Barbara Helfgott Hyett (1996)

Peasants Wake for Fellini's *Casanova* and
Other Poems
*Andrea Zanzotto; edited and translated by
John P. Welle and Ruth Feldman; drawings
by Federico Fellini and Augusto Murer*
(1997)

Moon in a Mason Jar and *What My
Father Believed*
Robert Wrigley (1997)

The Wild Card: Selected Poems,
Early and Late
*Karl Shapiro; edited by Stanley Kunitz
and David Ignatow* (1998)

Turtle, Swan and *Bethlehem in Broad
Daylight*
Mark Doty (2000)

Illinois Voices: An Anthology of
Twentieth-Century Poetry
Edited by Kevin Stein and G. E. Murray
(2001)

On a Wing of the Sun
Jim Barnes (3-volume reissue, 2001)

Poems
*William Carlos Williams; introduction by
Virginia M. Wright-Peterson* (2002)

Creole Echoes: The Francophone Poetry
of Nineteenth-Century Louisiana
*Translated by Norman R. Shapiro;
introduction and notes by M. Lynn Weiss*
(2003)

Poetry from *Sojourner:* A Feminist
Anthology
*Edited by Ruth Lepson with Lynne
Yamaguchi; introduction by Mary
Loeffelholz* (2004)

Asian American Poetry: The Next
Generation
*Edited by Victoria M. Chang; foreword by
Marilyn Chin* (2004)

Papermill: Poems, 1927–35
*Joseph Kalar; edited and with an
Introduction by Ted Genoways* (2005)

The University of Illinois Press
is a founding member of the
Association of American University Presses.

———————————————————————

Composed in 11/14 Adobe Garamond
with Adobe Garamond display
at the University of Illinois Press
Designed by Dennis Roberts
Manufactured by Thomson-Shore, Inc.

University of Illinois Press
1325 South Oak Street
Champaign, IL 61820-6903
www.press.uillinois.edu